Note From The Author

One message w
during our presentation coaching se...
"Less is More." In other words, say it and move on. As Voltaire said: "To be boring is to leave nothing out."

So, when I decided to write a book, I took on board that one message. I reckoned that the vast majority of our readers would have one thing in common – that they would be very busy - and therefore wouldn't have the time to read a 200 page tome.

Therefore, like all content, we've kept it short and to the point, focusing on the techniques that will really make a difference. Everyone who reads this should find at least three nuggets that they can store away and use next time they want to be an Impact Presenter.

I couldn't have written this without the help and support of fellow Amberites Paul, Richard and Liz, and a big thank you to them as well as to Jess at Zest who did the design.

But most of all thank you to all the numerous people who have been on our presentation courses and who encouraged me to write this.

Without that encouragement it simply wouldn't have happened.

Enjoy!

Ken

Published by
The Amber Group,
7 Great Lime Kilns,
Southwater,
West Sussex,
RH13 9JL, UK.

No part of this publication may be reproduced without the permission of The Amber Group.

Designed by www.alittlezest.com

Original text © 2012 The Amber Group
Revised 2024

www.ambergroup.co.uk

About The Author

Ken Deeks has been a presentation coach for over 20 years.

Previously a journalist before moving into in-house and agency PR, Ken has spent his entire career helping companies and individuals to deliver compelling content in a way that creates positive impact.

The Amber Group provides leadership, management and communications training and coaching to corporate teams and creative agencies. Set up in 2009 by Ken and fellow directors Paul, Richard and Liz, The Amber Group's training and coaching services are practical, effective and intrinsically linked to the improved performance of our clients' business today and in the future.

Ken is also the founder of Boycott Your Bed, previously known as Byte Night, the charity sleepout that has raised over £15 million for children's charity Action for Children (AfC). Ken was awarded an MBE in 2015 for his services to charity. Ken is also a VP at AfC and part of the proceeds of the sale of this book will go to the charity.

Contents

1. **Introduction**
   It's not natural
   The 3 whys men...
   I'm a nervous wreck - I just can't do it!

2. **Thinking Ahead**
   The Boring stuff - but boy is it important!
   Organisation
   Audience
   Venue and equipment
   You

3. **Building the Content**
   It must be relevant
   Start with the objectives
   Presentation Scoping

4. **Golden Rules for Building Content**
   Talk normal and keep it simple - stupid!
   Cut it out!
   Make it personal
   Colour it in
   The power of three

5. **Turning Words into a Presentation**
   Don't let the slides take over
   Less is more
   Rehearse, rehearse, and then rehearse...

6. **Delivering Your Presentation**
   Be YOU!
   Notes or no notes
   Variety is the spice of life
   Signposting - this way!
   The new comedy duo - Speed and Pace
   Emphasise
   Be an energy generator
   Making the slides work for you

   The Power of Stories in our Presentations
   Handling questions
   After the show

7. **Presenting Online**

8. **Summary**

1. Introduction

Being able to present is no longer a nice-to-have skill, it's a must have.

Rightly or wrongly we live in an age where the ability to communicate is often as important as the content we are communicating.

This applies to all walks of life, but particularly in services industries where what you are fundamentally selling is "you" – whether that be in finance, marketing, law or even software services. There is no product to hide behind – the presentation of "you" is what makes you buyable.

And presentations can take all forms. It can be to a group of 5 in a small meeting room to a presentation in front of 500 people at a theatre. It can be a presentation to secure a job; it can be to persuade a group of people that your view is a correct one; or it can simply be to win a new services contract.

It can also be delivered through various media. It can be face-to-face, via on-line platforms like Teams or Zoom, or even a faceless conference call where the ability to get your message across is as equally important but in someways far more difficult.

And then there are the ways that presentations can be used. Organisations are now using You Tube or video clips on their websites to get messages across, and in this way presentations can be viewed time and time again.

Whatever it is, it is difficult to progress in the world of business if you are unable to present effectively. That may seem unfair, but it's reality and so we just have to learn to live with it.

This means that to progress we have to learn and develop this skill. Presenting effectively will enable you to compete. But if you want to win then you have to stand out, you have to present with Impact. In other words you need to learn to be able to deliver Impact Presentations. Because if you do, then you will be creating your own IP – something that is unique to you and something that people want to buy.

1.1 It's not natural

How many times have you heard the words: "They're a natural presenter." to describe someone who's just given a very polished, entertaining and engaging presentation?

Quite a few times we would imagine.

Now, most presentation training books will probably tell you that the idea of a "natural" presenter is a myth; that all effective presenters have been well trained and that absolutely everyone can do it.

Well, I disagree.

I believe there is such a thing as a "natural" presenter in the same way that there is a 'natural' story teller or a natural joke teller.

These people are just inherently good at it; they've been born with it. They will always get a 9 or even a 10 out of 10.

But that doesn't mean to say that less natural presenters can't emulate what it is that those natural presenters do. Even if it is natural, there must be techniques they are using that make their presentations stand out.

This book is designed for those people that need to understand what those techniques are, so that they can put them into practice in order to be a more effective presenter – whether that's presenting a new proposal to a team of 5 or speaking at a conference to 200.

These techniques we will be uncovering extend beyond delivery – there are techniques that help to prepare; techniques to help you build the content, and techniques to help you rehearse.

Like all good training courses, this book is designed for you to digest the 3 or 4 nuggets that enable you to improve. It won't take a 5 out of 10 presenter to 10 – but it will take you to a 7 or an 8.

You might not turn out to be that natural presenter that you'd like to be. But you'd be close. And that's my promise.

1.2 The 3 whys men.......

As you approach any presentation, there will be one obvious question that you will be asking yourself: "Why am I doing it?"

So, why are you doing it?

It could be a whole stack of different scenarios. It might be a sales pitch; an update; some research you want to share. It could even be a presentation to secure a job.

But whatever the scenario, **there must be a defined objective** to why you are doing it? And every presentation should start with that question, finish with that question, and have that first "why" question running all the way through it.

If the point of the sales presentation is to win some business then every word, every graphic, every hand signal, every eye contact should be focused on that reason. If it doesn't help you with the defined objective – to win that piece of business – then don't do it.

The same rule applies to getting that job, sharing research etc.

However, there are two other Whys that you should be asking yourself – and they are connected to the first 'why'.

"Why" number two is**: "Why does it need to be presented?"**

When you think about it, you can apply for a job over the phone. You can do a sales pitch by sending a document over e-mail.

So, there must be a reason "why" you are having to **present** the information. Typically it's for two reasons. Firstly, because **you** want or need to.

Or secondly, because the **audience** wants you to. So, why do **you** want to or why do **they** want you to?

Perhaps it's because you need to persuade. Or add extra detail; maybe some added value. Or it's possibly because the audience wants to get a feel for you, your personality and your ability to deliver compelling content. They have a need, for whatever reason, to identify and understand your own unique IP.

Again, this second "why" needs to be considered as part of your preparation.

The third "why" is "why you"? Why have you been chosen to do this as opposed to anyone else? Is it because you have a particular skill? Some knowledge that you have that no-one else has? Or would it look strange if someone else on your team did it instead of you?
This is a critical question that you need to ask yourself because if you can't answer it then maybe someone else should be doing the

presentation.

Indeed, if you can't answer any of those 3 whys you probably need to rethink why you are doing this at all.

In summary, next time you need to present, consider the 3 whys. This will help you to prepare a far more effective presentation. One that will have Impact.

1.3 I'm a nervous wreck – I just can't do it!

There was a piece of research conducted recently in which participants were asked to list their greatest fears. Unsurprisingly the usual suspects were in the top 10 – spiders, heights, enclosed spaces.

And right there at number one was our old favourite, Speaking In Public, or SIP as we shall now call it.

But what got our attention was the number two spot.

Apparently our second greatest fear after SIP is a fear of DYING! Yep, we would rather die than speak in public!

Now we know that's nonsense but it gives you

some idea about how we feel about SIP. What I like about this research is that it shows that it's not a particularly exclusive club. Indeed everyone who presents will feel some kind of nerves before they go on stage.

A few years ago, I was in the audience to see an internationally well known golfer speak at a business conference.

The previous day he'd won a major tournament. Imagine what that must have been like; standing over a ball, keeping still, maintaining the quality of his stroke, knowing that he was being watched by thousands on the course and millions around the world on TV. Go forward about 15 hours and he's the guest speaker at a conference with about 200 people in the room. He was late coming on stage by about 20 minutes. It turned out that he was vomiting in the restroom because he was just so petrified at the thought of having to speak to 200 people.

So, if you're scared, then you aren't alone. But what can you do about it? There are numerous techniques that various presenters employ to overcome nerves.

They range from deep breathing and standing

with your legs wide – *remember former politician George Osborne at the Conservative Party conference in 2015?* - to staring at the back of the room and not at the people in it. Some people like a podium to lean against – it makes them feel hidden – while others like an autocue to make sure they don't slip up or freeze. Personally, I like to engage in conversations with the audience before I go on stage; that way I have got used to the sound of my own voice and the presentation feels like an extension of the conversation that's already underway.

But our personal favourite of all time is this: just do it!

It really is that simple – MAKE YOURSELF DO IT! Because the more you do it, the more used to it you become and, as a result, less nervous.

But make it easy for yourself. Make sure your first presentations are to small groups of friendly people, perhaps an internal team. Do that a few times. Then volunteer to present to a larger group, maybe 20 people. Then 30, 40, then 50. Then an audience that doesn't know you so well.

Suddenly the nerves won't be as bad and before you know it, you'll find yourself speaking at Wembley Arena. What an Impact Presenter you've become!

2.0 Thinking Ahead

The Boring Stuff – but boy is it important!

Before you even begin to think about preparing the content for the presentation, you need to think about the boring logistical stuff. Actually we shouldn't see it as boring because if you can get the logistics sorted and out of your head, then your mind is cleared to focus on the important things – like content and delivery.

How many times have you woken up during the night before a presentation worried about whether or not there's a microphone, or whether you've charged the laptop, or renewed your Zoom licence?

Well, if you haven't, I certainly have! That is, until I decided that the best way to avoid sleepless nights is to have a checklist.

However, there are a number of things you need to think about before we even get to the technology bit, and we've divided these into 4 sections – the organisation; the audience; the venue; and you!

2.1 Organisation

So, who is organising the event that you are speaking at – and why? Is it an events company i.e. someone whose primary revenue model is hosting paid-for events, or is it an event being put on by a company whose primary revenue model is something else e.g. a publishing house? Of course if it's an internal event or a business pitch then this part of the preparation is less important. However, if it's a "proper" conference then there are things you need to know.

First of all, why is the conference happening, other than, of course, to make money for the organisers? Clearly you need to know why you are speaking but what is the OVERALL theme of the event; why do they think that people will be attracted to it? In other words, **what is its primary objective?**

The next thing you need to consider is who the other speakers are and the topics they are planning to cover off. This is critical. There is nothing worse than standing on the sidelines, waiting to go on, and listening to the speaker before you cover off a similar topic and making the same points.

On this basis find out who is speaking directly before or after you. Is the ordering deliberate? Again, this would increase the need to find out what they are planning to say.

Indeed, the running order is something you need to consider to make sure you get a decent slot. If it's an all day event, try to avoid the usual grave yard slot straight after lunch. An even better slot to miss is the last one of the day. The attendees will now be restless, and half of them would have left for home (one of the accepted perks of being at a conference is that you get home early), so you'll be presenting to a half-empty room of people checking their mobile phones....

Any slot other than those are acceptable.

2.2 Audience

So, just who are these people who are planning to put 30 minutes or so of their lives in your hands? Strange to say but most presenters rarely think about this as much as they should mainly because they tend to focus more on themselves and how they are likely to come across.

The first thing you need to understand is the

profile of the audience, and then put yourself in their shoes. Who are they? How do they make a living? What roles do they have? What are their day-to-day and long-term challenges?

Most importantly – **and, boy, this is important** - what do they want from you? How can you help them? Because that's what they want from you; they want to gain knowledge or insight to help them to be better at their job.

Then you need to know how many. Are there 20 people in the room or 200? This is important as it will enable you to plan engagement techniques like audience interaction, and the way you do this will be different depending on the numbers of people in your audience.

Another consideration is whether your attendees are there under coercion (e.g. a management directive or a team building exercise). Also, find out whether they have paid to attend or whether it's free.

Paid for or free is an interesting one. It would be easy to think that just because it's free, the audience will be a softer touch than the audience that has paid - that expectations will be lower. I'm not convinced of that. Increasingly business people are conscious of the value of time, so therefore don't waste their time!

Indeed, people who have paid to attend are sometimes more accommodating; somehow they need to justify spending the company's money and are therefore "willing" the presenters to be good.

2.3 Venue & equipment

Impact Presenters are at their best when they are at their most confident. As well as being clear about who the audience is and what they want, our IP will gain confidence from having a clear idea of what the venue looks like.

So, as part of your prep, you need to ask the following questions:

What's the seating plan?
This will partly depend on numbers, of course, but the room can be arranged in a number of different ways: seating around individual tables; classroom or lecture style; horseshoe. This is important as part of your presentation should involve some interaction and you need to 'picture' it beforehand.

Visualising yourself delivering your presentation

will give you the confidence to do it.

How big is the room?
In other words, will you have to project your voice or "shout" as we prefer to call it. And if you have to shout then should you be asking for a microphone?

Is there a stage or are you on the same level as the audience?
Being on a stage gives you the opportunity to pace across; being on the same level gives you the opportunity to walk into the audience. Both are effective engagement techniques but you need to know beforehand which one you will use.

Will you be behind a lectern?
If so, how do you move away from it? A lectern, while giving a sense of safety, can often act as a barrier between you and the audience, and you should try and minimise the amount of time you stand behind it.

Is the technology set up so that you can press the button and away you go?
For some people, the thought of moving the mouse to find the right icon on their laptop – with an audience of 200 watching – can be

sickening.

The fear of technology malfunction is a hundred times worse if you are doing this online. For important presentations I've had my IT guy Pete in the room with me. He's my safety net if something goes wrong.

So, sort it out beforehand, enabling you to focus 100% on your content and how to deliver it in an impactful way.

In other words, get rid of the clutter!

2.4 You

There a couple of things to do with You. Firstly, the overall role you play at the event; and secondly, what you look like.

As far as your overall role is concerned, it goes much further than just doing your presentation. If you are at a conference, for example, make an effort to listen to other presentations, and to talk to some of the delegates during the breaks.

This could provide you with some material for your own presentation: *"I was talking to a couple of you during the break and was interested in some of the things that were said…"*

This makes it very personal to the audience and therefore more engaging. It makes it feel fresh and that much more relatable.

So, now to what you look like. How you dress matters. The important thing here is that you look comfortable, and the best chance of being comfortable is if you feel that the way you look mirrors your audience. If you're not sure then wear a suit – it is better to be slightly over dressed than under.

All of the above is more clutter in your head. Sort it out ahead of time so you can concentrate your efforts on content and delivery. Which is where we are going now.

Thinking Ahead: an event check list

Organisation:
- Who's organising the event and why?
- What's the theme of the event?
- What is its primary objective?
- Who are the other speakers and what are they speaking about?
- When are you speaking? Is there a clear order and is the order deliberate?
- Is it an internal or external event?
- Is it free or paid-for?

Audience:
- Who is in the audience? What's their profile?
- Why are they there?
- What do they want from you?
- How many of them are there?
- What do you want them to take away from your presentation?

Venue & Equipment:
- How is the seating organised?
- How big is the room?
- Is there a stage?
- Is there a lectern?
- Will you be wearing a microphone?
- How is the technology set up; and how do you interact with it?

3. Building the Content

3.1 It must be relevant

The first thing you need to think about when developing a presentation is the most obvious thing of all – it must be relevant to the audience.

A simple test of relevance is to think about the audience and why they are there. Their test will be: "What's in it for me?" If you can't answer that question then you need to re-think how you can!

3.2 Start with the objective

Return to that objective you identified in the preparation stage. What do you want to achieve? And what does your audience want to achieve?

Clearly these two need to be compatible. However you have an opportunity to steer them in the direction you want to go in.

To help with this, you need to identify the one key message that you want to deliver. Now the chances are there are a whole bunch of messages you'd like to get across. But as in the great speeches from people like Martin Luther King and Winston Churchill (see chapter 10), there was one critical message that they wanted their audience to take away with them

So, when you sit down to write your presentation, consider this: If someone who had been at your presentation was asked to describe what your presentation was about by someone who hadn't attended, what would you want them to say?

It's a technique we also advise for media spokespeople. All too often spokespeople engage in a journalist interview expecting to answer a bunch of questions on a specific topic – the Future of AI for example – without really properly considering the message they want to deliver.

So, in our media training sessions we advise spokespeople that as part of their preparation for a press interview, they write down the headline they'd like to see afterwards. And then everything you say to the journalist should be angled to achieve that headline.

Simple isn't it?

Now that you have your headline, the content

that creates it should form the spine of your presentation. And be shouted from the rooftops!

3.3 Presentation Scoping (PS)

Having identified the objective and checked to make sure it's relevant to your audience you now also need to scope the content of your presentation. Typically the content will consist of two elements – words and visuals.

This first part of this section will focus on the word; then we will deal with visuals.

So, how do we build the words?

The first thing you need to do is your Presentation Scoping (PS) by splitting your presentation into obvious "chapters".

For example, when you are writing a proposal you would usually build it along the following lines:

- introduction
- objectives
- strategy (to meet objectives)
- tactics (to implement strategy)
- results (or outcomes)

- cost
- conclusion

That's very neat; there's a clear path to the "story". And that is exactly how you need to build your presentation. So, for example if you were asked to deliver a presentation on the economy, it might look something like:

- introduction
- context (i.e. history or background)
- the state of the economy today
- why it's down the toilet
- what we do to get it out of the toilet
- our role in getting it out of the toilet
- what happens if we don't
- a call to action
- summary

Bingo – there's your presentation. So all you need to do is fill in the content to build your story and paint your picture. You have a framework and a clear spine which enables you to add the colour without straying from the point of your story.

This is important. The worst presentations are those that ramble all over the place; this in turn means that the audience is less clear about what you are trying to say; after a while they cease to care.

There are two aspects of PS that need further explanation – the introduction and the summary. These are your bookends and are in some ways the most important parts of the presentation; the former sets the scene, it explains why you are there and what you are planning to tell the audience. The latter is your opportunity to remind them about what they've heard and why it's important.

Introduction – this is when you tell them what you're going to tell them. In fact, you walk them through your PS headings. This is brilliant. The audience immediately gets a feel for the scope of your presentation and what you are going to cover. It's a bit like reading the back of a book before you buy it. It gives you enough to make you interested but without giving away the whole story.

The introduction also provides the opportunity to create some anticipation; to give some effective teasers. So, saying things like: *"..and while the economy is firmly down the toilet I do believe there is a way out but – and this is important – it is the people in this room that can make it happen. Later on I will tell you how. You may be surprised when I share it with you."*

Right, so now they *really are* listening. First of all you told them that you are going to share something new – and people love "new" – but you've also told them that it is very clearly to do with them.

The introduction will also enable you to express an opinion and explain that your presentation will seek to build a picture that persuades the audience that your opinion is the correct one: e.g. *"I firmly believe that the UK economy will head up all the economies across Europe and my presentation today will explain why I hold that belief."*

Throughout this, you are creating audience engagement – **it is about them.**

The Summary – your audience won't listen to every word you say. Have you ever been to a presentation and *not* found your mind wandering? Whether it's to do with those e-mails you need to send at the break or re-living your team's match at the weekend, you cannot listen to one person speaking solidly for 30 minutes.

As an Impact Presenter this reality may hurt but you have to accept it. And that's why the summary is so important as it enables you to ensure that YOUR audience takes away the important points that you wanted to make. So, don't be scared of repeating yourself.

Finish by saying: *"and so to summarise, here are the 3 things I want you to take away from my presentation."* And then list them: 1, 2 and 3. Ah, the power of 3 – we will come to that later.

You have now scoped out your presentation and you need to put the flesh on the spine by adding the words that you want to deliver.

As you do this, think of the golden rules that an Impact Presenter always follows. They are covered in the next chapter.

4. Golden Rules for Building Content

Rule Number One...

4.1 Talk normal and keep it simple – stupid!

If we really want to impress ourselves, and not the audience, then make simple things sound complicated.

But on the basis that it's the audience we want to impress, then let's keep it simple. Why say: *"These grants will incentivise administrators and educators to apply relevant metrics to assess achievements on the competencies they seek to develop."* When it is much easier for the audience to digest: *"Grants would be used to pay teachers who agreed to test their students."*

And what on earth was Meg Whitman, former head honcho at eBay thinking of when she said that she was *"encouraged by the fundamentals that underline usage growth of the net"* when she could have just said that she was happy that more people are using the internet.

You really don't have to speak like a management consultant to impress your audience. Just talk normal!

Golden Rule Number Two!

4.2 Cut it out!

Less is more: *"The best way to be boring is to leave nothing out."* Voltaire

I don't usually find myself quoting French philosophers but I reckon Voltaire was pretty spot on with this particular observation.

Have you ever left a presentation and thought *"that was too short!"*?

The trouble is we often want to say far too much and usually end up boring our audiences. Even more dangerous is that by saying too much we fail to get our key message across; because we dilute it.

The trick is to say what you need to say and move on, without repeating yourself by saying the same thing in a slightly different way.

So, when you've pulled together your content, look at what you plan to say and ask yourself this question about each sentence: *"If I take this sentence out will it have an adverse impact on the presentation?"* If the answer is a resounding "no" then whip it out.

Golden Rule Number Three

4.3 Make it personal

And so it should be; after all, why are you there if it isn't.

Impact Presenters recognise that effective presentations need to be personalised – after all that is their IP. You can do this in a number of ways.

First, don't be frightened to give your opinion: *"So, what this tells me is that….."* or *"My take on this is that…"*

Secondly, involve the audience: empathise with them; get them on your side: *"So, why should this be important to you?"* or *"I know that right now you are sitting there thinking that if we…."*

Thirdly, tell anecdotes about yourself: *"On the way to this presentation, I bumped into someone from the audience. We then had a conversation about X and I made the point…"*

Doesn't it feel so much more conversational?

Doesn't it feel like you are all in this together?

Making it personal will help you to engage that much more with the audience.

Golden Rule Number Four

4.4 Colour it in

Most presenters are lazy. Typically their objective is to get through it. Very few think about making their presentations entertaining and evocative.

I regularly ask people who their favourite presenters are and I'm not surprised when the name Stephen Fry is mentioned. This is a 'presenter' who wouldn't dream of using a lazy word. Every word is considered carefully and then delivered lovingly. He would never use 'lovely' when 'sumptuous' would work so much better.

Look for the high energy and serious, considered points in your presentation and adapt your presentation style, tone and pace to reflect them. For example, if you are selling a big idea or trying to paint a picture for the audience, use colourful language and become more energised and animated in the way you present. The audience will feed off your enthusiasm. If you are making a serious consultative point, slow your speed right down and leave more deliberate pauses between each point to emphasis the importance.

This is also an opportunity to be the real 'you.' Don't be scared to tell a story, an anecdote, something about you that adds flavour to the presentation and supports the theme you are addressing. It also provides an opportunity for audience participation; ask the audience questions, encourage them to tell their stories, make them feel that they are PART of YOUR presentation. Do that and they will be eating out of your hands.

Golden Rule Number 5

4.5 The power of 3

It has been proved that we can easily remember 3 things. More than that and people start to forget.

So, consider ordering your presentation in 3's. That can mean 3 parts to the presentation itself, or 3 key takeaways, or 3 bullets on each slide.

Clearly this shouldn't be overly manipulated –

after all there might be 4 critical observations you want to make – but keep it in mind. It does work.

5. Turning Words Into A Presentation

5.1 Don't let the slides take over

You now have the words you want to use to present your story.

You then have to take those words and find a way of presenting them as a visual aid – this is usually in the form of a PowerPoint, Prezi or Canva document.

Your presentation can go one of two ways depending on what role you think your visual aid plays.

A lazy presenter will see the visual aid as a crutch for their own presentation. They will fill the slides full of words because that means they can read off the slides and don't have to rehearse much - which makes for a poor presentation.

An Impact Presenter, however, understands that a slide full of words will cause some real problems with the audience. That's because the human brain can't cope with having to listen to someone speaking while reading text at the same time. Try reading a book and listening to your partner telling you about their day, both at the same time. See, can't be done!

And that's what lazy presenters are fundamentally asking you to do when they bring up a slide with lots of words which they then start talking to.

The audience tries to listen while reading and then chooses one over the other – or gives up on both.

So, the point here is that your slides are there to support your delivery, not compete with it. They should complement what you say, not dominate. How many people say they are going to a conference to read some slide decks? Of course they don't; they say they are going to hear some speakers.

Having established the role of the slide, we need to establish what goes on it.

Your slides should be created with reference to your Presentation Scope (PS). From the PS, you should be able to take the words you are planning to say, establish the key point and identify the evidence statements you are using to support that key point. This is called framing and is covered again in section 6.8.

5.2 Less is more

For example, let's say that the presentation words you want to say are:

"There are three reasons why the economy is in trouble. The first reason is because of the initial problems caused by the sub prime market in the US. The second reason is because of the on-going crisis impacting the economies of several countries in the Euro zone. And the third reason is because the UK failed to spot what was going on early enough and took too long to take corrective action."

Now, you could have these 3 as bullets on a slide, as below:

There are 3 reasons why the economy is in trouble:

- firstly, initial problems caused by the sub prime market in the US

- secondly, the on-going crisis impacting on the euro-zone

- thirdly, UK banks etc. failed to see the problem and react quickly enough and leave the audience to battle over whether or not they should listen to you or read the slides. Or, you could have a slide that reads:

Economic crisis. Why?
US – sub-prime
Europe – eurozone
UK – too slow

The audience will take 3 seconds to take in that snap shot, lean back and then listen to their Impact Presenter.

Not only that, it provides plenty of space for ONE highly impactful graphic. In this case it could be a globe with danger lightning bolts exploding from the 3 regions.

The above approach is one that we would suggest in a perfect world. However, being ever practical, we do accept that from time to time, and in different circumstances there may be a need to provide more information on a slide. For example, this could be where the presentation itself has to double up as a report or a proposal.

However, there are obvious ways round this. Firstly, the report can be provided as a PowerPoint but with the content in the notes section.

Secondly, to ensure that the words aren't being read before you've even started to present that particular slide, use animations (or builds or reveals as they are also known) to open up new bullets as you get to them.

5.3 Rehearse, rehearse, and then... rehearse.

And then stop.

It is important to rehearse even if it's just for logistical reasons. Obviously you need to know that what you are saying fits the time you've been allocated. No-one will thank you for overrunning, the organisers won't and the delegates certainly won't. Have you ever left a presentation thinking that it was too short?

You also need to check that it flows and the right messages are being delivered.

Rehearse in front of the mirror, or even film yourself and play it back. We always film delegates on our presentation training courses because we know that the vast majority of them will be pleasantly surprised by what they see.

If you have written out your presentation in full, never try to learn it parrot fashion. This can lead to freezes on stage when your brain forgets what followed on from the last line. Instead, take each section and dilute it down to your key points and then jot down one trigger word to remind you of each point – ideally these will be the trigger words on your slide. Then rehearse the presentation aloud until you are comfortable that you understand the key point you want to make for each trigger word.

The important thing here is to rehearse it aloud. And the reason for this is because when we speak we use much simpler language and sentence construction than when we write. If you try to speak out loud the words you originally wrote down, it will sound awkward and contrived and we want you to speak naturally and with impact.

But here's some advice you won't often hear; don't rehearse too much! You can be overly slick; and the odd stutter here, or an unplanned pause while you collect your thoughts can be incredibly endearing to an audience that wants to hear from a fellow human being and not a robot.

6. Delivering Your Presentation

It's now time to deliver your presentation. You've done all the preparation, you've built the content, you've rehearsed in front of the mirror. Now it's show time!

And to be honest that's really how you should look at it. Impact Presenters know they are there to put on a show. Clearly the content is the most important part of any presentation but quite often it's the delivery that people remember. A combination of compelling content and engaging delivery will keep them asking for more.

The very first thing you need to establish is that YOU are in control. In control of yourself and in control of the audience.

When you stand up, the audience typically relinquishes control to you. If you don't lead, they feel uncomfortable, so the secret is showing control and leadership at all times.

Clearly it is easier to say this than do it. If you are particularly nervous then concepts like 'leadership'; and 'control' will feel particularly daunting. However there are a number of techniques you can use to put yourself in control, and enable yourself to deliver your content with impact.

6.1 Be YOU!

To be in control you need to be you. We will always have our favourite presenters, whether that's Michelle Obama, Tony Blair or Winston Churchill, but please, please do not try to be them. Sure, learn from their techniques, but that should be as far as it goes.

As soon as you walk on to the stage, or stand up at the head of the room, and open your mouth, the audience will be making a rapid judgement. And one of the first things they will be judging is authenticity. Are you authentic? Are you you; or are you trying to be someone else? Remember the politician William Hague wearing a baseball cap back to front at the Notting Hill Carnival? What on earth possessed him or his advisers? He was rightly ridiculed because it wasn't authentic.

Therefore, if your natural style is loud, be loud; if it's quiet then be quiet. You don't have to be loud to put on a show you just need to have variety in your delivery (see chapter 4).

So, to be in control, be authentic.

6.2 Notes or no notes?

Of course it is always more impactful if you can stand up there and deliver your presentation without notes. It is impressive and gives you added credibility.

So, to be an Impact Presenter with total control over your audience, don't use notes.

However, we do recognise that presenters with limited experience are still building their confidence and it is important that you don't do anything to negatively impact on that confidence.

There are 3 stages presenters typically go through as they develop their skills and techniques through increased experience:

Firstly – they have their full set of notes in front of them and they read off them.

Secondly – they have some headers or pointers, or key messages for each slide, which helps to keep them on track.

Thirdly – present without any notes at all.

I would suggest that, even if you're not a seasoned presenter, you should try and go straight to stage 2.

By having some notes in front of you, you are at least able to follow your own story. Our biggest fear, as presenters, is that we forget where we are with our story and we dry up as our brain decides to shut down. Having our one takeaway message for each slide provides the confidence to know that we will have something to say, even if we are not talking to the whole slide – which might not be a bad thing anyway.

6.3 Variety is the spice of life

The dullest presentations we've sat through are the ones that lack variety. Flat delivery, slides that look the same etc.

Variety will alter how your presentation is received.

So, think about what that variety – that change – might look like.

It could be a switch in volume and tone, or a change in pace –

one minute quick, the next minute s-l-o-w-i-n-g d-o-w-n…….thenspeedingitupagain……

A word that's *SHOUTED* can drag the audience out of its stupor. But so can silence. Indeed, a pause of 5 seconds will have everyone listening because total silence is not what they expect at a presentation.

What else can we vary? Well, why not move around. We're not talking about the dancing on the spot you sometimes get – and how irritating is that! No, what we are talking about are deliberate movements to re-enforce critical points – like walking to the slide to point out a significant statistic or walking into the audience to stress a key point.

And then there's the use of hands. Waving them around pointlessly is, well, pointless. But using hands to accentuate critical observations will really help to keep the audience engaged. And remember, the bigger the audience, the more deliberate and bigger the movements need to be to be recognised by the people at the back of the room.

Also remember eye contact is important to keep the audience engaged. Make sure that as you talk you look around the room, catching the eye of one section of the audience for just a second before moving onto the next. This approach will ensure that the audience stays focused on you and what you are saying. And even in a very large audience it works just as well. Just pick a spot on the left, centre and right of the room and move your attention between the three spots during your presentation. As humans, we are all vain and even in a large crowd when somebody looks our way we will feel that they are looking straight at us!

6.4 Signposting – this way!

It is important that your audience is able to follow the path to your destination. Remember when we did our Presentation Scope (PS) in the preparation stage (see **section** 3.3)? Well we need to communicate those to the audience at the beginning, during and at the end of our presentation.

This helps our audience to know where we are at any stage of the presentation and understand both how we got there and where we are going next.

Agendas and agenda slides can help with this. So for audience members who have drifted off thinking about what to have for dinner, the re-emergence of an agenda slide is one way to get them back on track.

But the Impact Presenter also needs to verbalise this by pointing out where they are on the agenda and reminding the audience what has been covered off - and, importantly, where we are going next: For example: *"so that covers off the current situation and I would now like to share with you what I believe are the challenges moving forward. After this I will share with you what I think OUR role is in all of this. But next up – what are the challenges? Well, the challenges are these:....."*

Don't be frightened to over-egg it – your audience will be grateful for any signposting or structure they can get.

6.5 The new comedy duo – Speed and Pace

Fact: Most presenters speak too quickly.

While it is important to vary your pace, speaking too quickly all the time is a presentation disaster. The human brain simply cannot take in many words in too few seconds. We also need to consider the increasingly international make-up of any business audience. I once spoke at a conference where the audience represented 17 different languages. Actually I just made that up – I haven't got a clue how many languages they spoke – but the point is you would believe it because it could be true. So while a non-native English speaker could probably understand the six words that make up the statement, *"the economy is down the toilet,"* they might struggle with the statement delivered as one word *"Theeconomyisdownthetoilet."*

And yet that is often how quickly we speak when presenting. Research suggests that when we present our pace is 50% faster than our normal speed. That's fast.

So, how do you overcome this? There are 3 techniques that work:

- Emphasis. By emphasising key words (or verbal underlining), elongating them as you say them and underlining them through the force of your voice.

- You will find that you naturally pause. This brings us onto pausing....

- Build in spaces for pauses. Even silences! This will help you to slow down.

- Think speed bumps. As you speak and as you feel yourself speeding up, visualise a speed bump ahead of you. This will help you to slow down as you approach the bump, then almost stop – but not quite – as you go over the bump, and then speed up again. This technique is also great for variety.

6.6 Emphasise

Verbal underlining gets a section of its own – because it is **<u>critically</u>** important.

When you read the sentence above, what word stood out? I imagine it was the word 'critically.' Why? Well, it's obvious; we put it in bold and underlined it. And you need to do the same when you say it instead of writing it.

Think about any conversation you have with a friend. If you're telling them a story there will be parts of the story that you want to stand out e.g. *"and guess how many eggs they put in that cake? Well, I'll tell you - they put in EIGHT, yes EIGHT eggs. No wonder it was so rich!"*

There is always a part of any story that you want to stand out. So, make it stand out. You can do this through a number of different techniques:

- ask a question that you are not expecting them to answer, and then answer it yourself: *"So have you any idea what kind of debt we are talking about?"*

- pause before giving an answer

- use emphasis words before delivering important messages: words like *"critically" "importantly"* and *"crucially"* are great emphasis words. Use them at the beginning of a sentence and then pause. Your audience will hang on every word.

6.7 Be an energy generator

Energy is infectious. If you are energetic then the chances are that your audience will respond accordingly.

You can display energy in all sorts of ways. Body movement is an obvious one. Energy in your voice will make a difference. But don't forget deliberate eye contact. Move your eyes around the room and stop at different people for 3 seconds, before moving on again. It is a very powerful mechanism to keep your audience alert – and, importantly, to show that you are in control.

If you are sitting down in a meeting room, having the confidence to jump up and walk over to the screen or whiteboard to point out something on a chart or graph immediately draws the attention of the audience back to you and shows confidence and composure. These tactics, used sparingly, can be very effective.

Indeed, there is plenty of research that shows words alone aren't very persuasive. A piece of research you may already be familiar with is the one that says we need a combination of words, tone and body language to be able to persuade and of that mix, the most potent is body language (55%), tone (38%) and words (7%).

Personally I'm not convinced of those percentages but they do help us to consider what does influence an audience. Here's an experiment. Try saying *"I love you"* to your partner in the flattest, uninspiring tone imaginable. Yep, you got the stony look back as well!

Said with the right tone, with some energy in the tone AND in the way you express yourself – lots of arm movement - and you probably would have got a very different response.

Words provide the information. Tone makes it believable. Body language persuades and entertains. What a great mix!

6.8 Making the slides work for you

I have previously discussed the need for any slides to complement your delivery.

Slides are also a useful way of creating and maintaining control.

Firstly each slide should tell its own part of the story, with one particular message specific to that slide. You need to communicate this by framing the slide to give it context. When we normally communicate, we tell linear stories building to a punchline. For example, *"I woke up this morning, got out of bed, pulled back the curtains and it was a beautiful sunny day, so I bounced down the stairs with a spring in my step."* When we frame a slide we want to reverse this concept – giving the big message first and then supporting that open statement with the detail contained with the rest of the slide. The reason we take this approach is to help the audience to follow our story and take away the main points we want to make. Each time we change the slide, the audience naturally tunes back into our presentation, looks at the slide and will listen to our first few words. So, we need to make sure that those first few words are always the key ones we want the audience to take away.

One way of helping you, as the presenter to achieve this goal, is to make sure your heading for each slide is the key framing message you want the audience to take away. So, rather than a heading reading *"Challenge"* it might say *"Inertia is our big challenge"*.

However, despite the need to frame each slide you are still telling a story. Powerful storytellers are able to link the different strands to build overarching messages. So, while each slide does indeed tell part of the story, you will need to have techniques in place to ensure that you don't deliver a series of short stories.

Don't get me wrong, short stories are highly powerful – we call them impact vignettes – but only if they play a critical role in delivering the overall story or message.

One such technique is to build slide transitions. So, that as you conclude on one slide you are already using the words to link to the next slide e.g. *"So, if this slide is showing us what we need to do to get out of this economic mess, the next slide firmly illustrates the challenges that we will face in doing so."*

You will see from this example that you have delivered an obvious transition from one slide to the next, while at the same time providing both a summary of the previous slide and 'framing' words for the next slide.

This is hugely powerful storytelling and will give your presentation impact.

Storytelling can make a presenter stand out. So let's talk more some more about it.

The Power of Stories In Our Presentations.

There is a famous saying: *"Facts Tell, Stories Sell."*

When I first heard this, my initial understanding was that a presentation should focus purely on stories.

Now I know I'm wrong. You absolutely need both because it is the facts that will give evidence to the stories.

But it is often the stories that are the most memorable, and importantly, will form the content that is retellable!

Every organisation out there wants to talk about what their business does, and no doubt this will form part of your presentation. But if you tell stories that describe what your company does, then you are potentially giving your audience stories that they themselves can feel equipped to retell.

How powerful is this? It's why we coined the phrase **The Power of the Retellable Story**. And that's because if you have people out there – employees, clients, prospects, partners, media – retelling YOUR stories, then you are creating a whole community of individuals who are becoming promoters of your organisation.

For example, we work with companies who, while they have several brilliant stories about the difference they have made to their clients, they are only told by the people who are close to those stories, who probably worked on the projects themselves. We help them to cascade these stories around their organisation so fellow employees feel compelled to tell them to other audiences even though they weren't part of the team that delivered the project. How powerful is that?

So, what makes a retellable story?

Firstly, it needs to be easy to understand. Secondly, it should be relatable. Thirdly it must include all the key points – no 'reteller' wants to be asked crucial questions they can't answer. Fourthly, it should paint pictures, be visual. Finally, there needs to be an outcome or a result.

Let me give you a true example. A client was telling me about how they had helped a law enforcement agency to become more digitally enabled by building a secure back-office infrastructure. That's fine. Interesting. But would I have a desire to retell it? Nope!

He went onto expand on his story, explaining that his team had created an application that sits in the body cameras for police officers. Wow!

He then told it in a different way: "*Imagine you're a police officer on the beat. You're on your own. It's late at night. You turn the corner and there is an armed gang of youths coming towards you. The one thing that can save you is the camera. You can tell them they are being watched, that it's a live recording and that back-up is on its way."*

That's a quick retell but I bet you all visualised it, right? You saw a police officer, you saw a gang. They will probably look different to each of us, but we all have a picture in our head. How powerful is that? Oh, and by the way, the facts are that this app had massively reduced both attacks on and complaints against the police. What a brilliant story!

Now, one push back I get when I relay this example of a good story is that, for some people, they want to know about the process, they want to know the details of the technology. It's a reasonable push-back. Yes, some people in your audience may want that, but some may not – and the one thing I will say is that EVERYONE likes a story they can relate to. It might be the red-top tabloid version of the story but it's still compelling. Yes, the tech folk might want an *IT Today* version to add to their understanding but they are still likely to enjoy the *Sun* version, provided it contains enough content to make it retellable.

And what is it that makes it so retellable? It's because it's *relatable*. We have spent so many evenings watching fictional cop shows from the

Sweeney to Happy Valley and Line of Duty. We know the police, we know how it works, we can absolutely relate to it. How I know that is what makes it retellable is because two weeks after being told this story I was watching a documentary in which the videos of police chases were being filmed through body cameras. I turned to my kids and explained this is what one of my clients did. My eldest commented that this was the first time I'd ever told them about what my clients do! And that's because I had a retellable story.

Another aspect that makes a story relatable is location.

Rightly or wrongly we relate to stories that feel, well, local. A two-vehicle car crash in our road will be more relevant to us – and therefore a more interesting story - than a several-car pile-up in another part of the country. Again, rightly or wrongly, we will be more likely to retell a story we have heard on the news about two people being killed in a mudslide in Manchester than we would if the story was about 20 people killed in a mudslide in South America. It's simply because we can picture it more and it therefore becomes more relatable.

So, that's an example of a retellable story.

What else does a retellable story need. It needs to be NICE!

No, I'm not talking about Disney's Frozen. I'm introducing an acronym which will help you to focus on three key aspects you should always try to include.

The N stands for NEW. Your audience will want to hear new things. If it's not new – if they know it already – why would they want to listen? So, make sure you tell them something they didn't already know.

The I stands for IMPORTANT. If it's new because it is now available in a slightly different shade of red, then your audience is unlikely to be impressed or excited. But if the NEW thing will transform the way your customers engage with you, then your audience will be totally engaged. Now, I imagine that you are already including the NEW and the IMPORTANT in your new business pitches and presentations. But it's the C that's often gets overlooked.

The C stands for CLEVER – so, what is CLEVER about your NEW IMPORTANT thing or idea?

This is your uniqueness. Everyone else turns the

lever to the right but you and your team have worked out a way to turn it to the left – and that 'new way' will increase productivity by 50%. Only you know how to do that. That's why, dear prospect with lots of money, you need to work with me.

Ooh, nearly forgot the E. That NEW IMPORTANT CLEVER message needs to be delivered with all the EMPHASIS you can muster. That EMPHASIS – or verbal underlining, as we call it, will ensure that the main message lands.

Clever, isn't it? (Btw, we originally called it INC! Important, New, Clever! But thought we needed the EMPHASIS to include delivery. Hmmm, still not sure. Quite like INC!....)

Right, we now know what makes a RETELLABLE story.

But how do you go about telling it?

Well, you tell it using the same techniques we've already explored so far in this book.

First of all you need that headline in your head. Headlines are written to entice an audience to read the story. So, if you were writing my earlier policeman with body camera story for a newspaper, what would your headline be? Mine might have been: *"New App Saves Coppers' Lives."* If I saw this headline, I would want to read the story.

It's the same with a story in a presentation. Your headline should be delivered to make your audience want to hear your story.

Then onto your first couple of sentences. Again, like any presentation you need to create a desire to listen. And so you would pull out the key point and then build from there. Imagine you'd bumped into a Hollywood legend on the way to meeting your friends in the pub. You'd rush into the bar and shout about how you'd just met Brad Pitt!

You wouldn't say, for example: *"I left the house at 6.30 travelling down Overdown Road before getting in the number 8 bus etc etc...."* If you did then you'd probably find yourself at the bar on your own!

So, the story needs to start with the big bang and THEN build it back up with context and background.

There is an alternative here that I do need to mention. Let's say it was a B-list celeb that you met and not Brad Pitt. In that instance, you might say *"Guess who I just bumped into."* And have the name of the B-list celeb as a reveal at the end. It's the same as click-bait. Using this as an example, the headline would be *"Brad Pitt falls over on the Red Carpet."* That would be enough to make people want to click through to the story. If it's a B-list celeb then the headline is more likely to be *"Celeb falls over on the Red Carpet."* They want you to click through even though you might be slightly disappointed to find out that it wasn't someone that famous....

Final tip on story telling: Your story will be far more effective if it's about people – police on the beat, the lad from two doors down who broke his arm in the car crash, Brad Pitt!! And remember to tell people stories when you are pitching for new business. Sure, you can talk about how you have previously helped the IT department at Barclays Bank but how much more memorable would it be if you told them about the time you met Lisa, the new CTO at the bank; and how you walked into her office to find her with her head in her hands and she looked up and just said *"help.."?*

You pictured that, right? You saw Lisa. We all saw a different Lisa, but we saw someone who needed help – and if we were the prospect in this situation, then it is likely that Lisa is someone we could relate to.

Like presentations, a story has to have colour. It has to paint pictures that your audience can imagine and it has to be relatable. But it also needs to INCLUDE your audience, wherever possible. At our training workshops we run ice-breakers where we ask people to tell a story about themselves. But stories about ourselves can be boring to others. So, if I said that I wanted to tell you about my recent holiday to Norway, your hearts would sink. There's nothing more boring than someone telling you about their holiday!

But if I said: *"I want to tell you about my holiday to Norway because I think you would love it there,"* you are far more likely to be interested because you think the story is being told for YOU and not for the storyteller. Those 8 extra words can make all the difference.

The last thing is the length of the story. There is a famous saying: *"I wanted to write you a short letter but I didn't have the time so I've written you a long one instead."* The point here is that it is sometimes harder to leave stuff out, but we should try to make it as concise as possible. I do get this, but we are talking about stories here and stories will have colour and tensions and contrasts and unexpected parts to it. Sure, I could say: *"I met Brad Pitt,"* but you'd want to know where, what was he like, what was he wearing, did I chat to him etc. In other words, you haven't given your friends a retellable story. They don't feel equipped to tell a story about how their friend met Brad Pitt because they don't know the full story. They would be asked obvious questions they can't answer.

Storytelling methodologies? It's a mystery to me......

I'm often asked about methodologies around storytelling. Clearly there are core components and we have covered these in the main text; these include having a hook/headline, a basic structure, contrasts/surprises and people - heroes, villains, underdogs etc.

The Horizon IT Post Office scandal, which saw hundreds of post office managers imprisoned due to a technology glitch, and which has been described as the UK's greatest miscarriage of justice, is a classic story of our time and contains all of the above story components. But the story has been told in many different ways. It was first told by trade publication *Computer Weekly*, then by satirical mag *Private Eye*, then through the nationals – tabloid redtops and broadsheets – and finally through a TV drama series.

CW, for example, would have focused on the technology angle, the nationals on the injustice of a flawed system, and the TV series on the human drama. That isn't to say *CW* wouldn't have touched on the human drama or that the TV series wouldn't have covered the technology aspect, it's just that it would have been explored through different lenses based on their readership, their audience.

Think about your favourite books. In my top 50 I would have *Murder on The Orient Express* by Agatha Christie and *Emma* by Jane Austen. Both are just brilliant stories. But they are told in very, very different ways.

Both have all the components of a great story, but a common methodology for telling them? Well, I couldn't see one; and if it's there then, well, it's a mystery to me......

6.10 Handling Questions

The one area most presenters worry about is handling questions. This is the bit of the presentation that you can't script and therefore is the one part you can't control.

To help prepare for this, you need to put yourself in the shoes of the audience – indeed, as you should do with ALL communications.

So, think about the questions you would ask if you were in the audience. This is a helpful exercise in itself; if there are questions that you would obviously want to ask then perhaps they should already be answered in the presentation itself?

That aside, having thought of the obvious questions, practice the answers you should give.

Of course there are always questions that come up that you wouldn't have thought of. But typically the questions asked are unlikely to have a *"yes"* or *"no"* answer – typically it will be a request for your view. So, give it. Give it, in the same way that you would have given it if you'd been asked by friends in a pub. They might not agree with your answer but it's your view. And it's the view of an expert; an expert who has just given a presentation because they are an expert!

Most presenters then worry that their opinion is going to be challenged. But remember, the vast majority of the audience don't want to see an argument between two people. So, if the questioner challenges your answer then just suggest that you take the conversation off-line; that it's important that you take questions from other people in the audience. Deliver this message with confidence and with a smile. Demonstrate that you are in charge.

One other thing you need to consider is the length of the answer. Some presenters feel that a question is a challenge and therefore there is a requirement to persuade. But it isn't – typically it's just a question. Answer it and take another question. Don't feel the need to answer it one way, then another way and then yet another way. And don't say *"Does that answer your question?"* They may so 'no' and then you're into an unhelpful argument.

Three questions are reasonable. After that you can carry on or shut it down.

6.11 After the show

As an Impact Presenter who is always looking to improve, it is important that you get feedback – that's how you will continue to learn.

Feedback can often be direct and obvious. For example, if you win the contract that you're bidding for, and your presentation is part of that bid, then clearly you did ok.

Asking your team how you did rarely works – they will typically say you did well even if you didn't – after all what's in it for them to be truthful if you weren't great?

One technique is to hire an independent company to carry out win: loss audits. One of the questions they will ask your client (or lost prospect) is what they thought of the presentation; and they will then provide that honest feedback.

If you were speaking at a conference then typically they have feedback forms that the audience is asked to complete. If you have any say over the content of the forms ask the organisers to include a section for feedback from the audience on what you could have done to improve your presentation further.

If you score poorly then ask the organisers for some constructive feedback - you have the evidence to show that you weren't great so you're not asking them to deliver that particular piece of bad news, you just want some explanations – and help to get it right next time.

7.0 Presenting Online

Many presentations are now given online.

I've been thinking about how I cover this as a specific topic, as it's not wrong to say that everything else we've discussed in this book applies to online as well as face-to-face.

However, there are a several things we do need to think about.

One of the first things to think about is how we look. Camera position is critical here. If you know you will be presenting on camera for some time, it's worth moving your camera back to put you in waist-up frame (think News Reader) rather than having your face close-up. This allows your hand movement to be included in your delivery which helps to keep viewers focused for longer.

And then there's eye contact. Because you are on camera, everything is in hyperfocus, so the smallest expressions or distractions are exaggerated. Make sure your eye contact stays focused at your camera to make the audience feel like you are looking straight at them.

Another consideration is your background. Ooh

this one is a real dilemma. Do you want them to see the 'real' you, so family pics in the background amongst the obligatory bookshelves and the usual clutter? Or is it the corporate look with the logo and the meaningless corporate message about how you are inspiring the next generation through some innovative platform or another? (Why is everything on a platform these days. Seriously, 80% of the world's population still think a platform is something you stand on when waiting for your next train.) And then of course you can have the blurred screen behind you but I always think that means someone is hiding something…..

Tough one but I'd go corporate for the biggie and perhaps the blurred one for the more intimate presentations. But if you do go for the 'real you' be careful. Rows of books, for example, can be a distraction for the attendees who are suddenly fascinated by you taste in books, and are therefore not listening to you. And while this means you can have a subtle sell on the go – for example, several copies of The Little Black Book of Presentation Secrets on the bookshelf behind – try to avoid any stand out pictures, photos, awards mementos etc. If it reduces the focus on you then don't have it there. It's that simple.

One of the biggest challenges we face when presenting on-line is that, in contrast to in-person presentations, we often have to present to a bunch of empty squares on the screen.

If we aren't in a position to control this – by, for example, asking people to put on their cameras - we have to get on with it, knowing that we can't read the room, we can't see how people are reacting to what we are saying, we can't even get that interaction that we may well get if it's face-to-face.

This means that at times we have this horrible feeling that our audience just isn't listening; that they are doing other things; that they may indeed have left the room to make a coffee!

The answer to this is to exaggerate the techniques we would use to gain attention in a usual presentation. For example, verbal underlining has to go to a new level. One 'importantly' followed by a pause just won't be enough. You'll need at least three! Seriously, try it! It will feel odd but it works. " *Importantly. Seriously, this is important. The next bit is something so important that you really have to listen. It will save your life!*" Ok, you might not need the last one, but you get my point.

Pausing and voice projection will also make a difference.

Another tip to get attention is to ask someone a question. Call out their name. Do this early on. For example: *"Actually Bob, is this something you're seeing in the market?"* No doubt there will be a crashing sound as Bob turns off his mute and says: *"Sorry Jane, I didn't quite hear that, can you repeat the question please?"*

But after that, everyone else on the call will be very attentive.....

Or if you think that's a tad unfair then drop Bob a note ahead of the meeting telling him you will be asking him to expand on the latest sales figures early in the call. It will still have the same effect – after all, no-one will know that you've tipped off Bob in advance.

Then there's the slides. Let's just say your audience has been distracted. Maybe they had to take a doorstep delivery from Amazon and they've come back to their laptop. They are looking at your slide and they are trying to work out which bit you are talking about. They feel lost. So, this is where brilliant and clear slide navigation comes in. Say things like: *"I now want to draw your attention to the second bullet in the orange box halfway down the left column on the slide, the one that says……..."*

As a member of your audience, I would love that you have been so thoughtful.

My other tip is to make sure you are 'in the room' 10 minutes before you need to present. This will give you the opportunity to engage in conversations as people join. This can be the usual small talk or even a quick update on a business issue. All you are doing here is repeating what you would do face-to-face but it's something we are less inclined to do on an on-line call – somehow a remote meeting seems more formal.

But what it does do is help to build your confidence as a presenter. You can hear your own voice as you chat to other people so that when you do start to present it can feel like an extension of the conversation, rather than an awkward silence with a silent drum-roll in your head – all of which will add to the already existing tension.

Don't get me wrong, you still need to adopt your presentation persona but it will feel less like the big one-person show that can you feel that much more comfortable.

So, have that chat!

8.0 Summary

So, now you are ready to present.

I hope you'll agree that we've covered a lot in just a few pages.

We've certainly looked at how we need to prep. We've considered the content and how to make it impactful. We've discussed techniques you can use to command the attention of your audience both visually and through the words you use. We've even looked at how you deal with questions.

But most importantly we've looked at how you MUST be you.

You are unique. There is no-one else like you. You indeed have your very own IP. You therefore need to use that unique IP to be an Impact Presenter.

Try to be someone else and you will fail.

Be you. Be good. No, be brilliant! Go for it!

Printed in Great Britain
by Amazon